Justice S. D. J.

Thank you for your support. Stay Well

Melinda Pruitt

I Choose You...
From One Thousand Babies

Storybook and Photo Album

By Melinda J. Pruitt

Art by Samantha Gustafson

This
Storybook and Photo Album
is dedicated to my sons,
Levon and Nadir.

I love you,
Mommy

Introduction

Remember hearing a song or reading a greeting card and thinking that song, that card says exactly what I wanted to say. This storybook/photo album has been written based on that same premise. This storybook speaks of your love for your baby and captures special moments of your child's birth and growth.

As a new mom, the first time I saw my new born, I thought that God had given me the prize of all prizes, the baby of all babies. I knew I had the most beautiful, most perfect baby in the world. I would tell my baby, if God let me choose from 1000 babies I would choose you. When my second baby was born I had that same feeling of joy and awe. I knew that feeling of joy and awe was universal, felt by moms and dads all over the world.

The concept of this book, is to have parents capture special moments through photos and add them to the storyline. As a keepsake this storybook/photo album would become a very special gift, given to your child when they grow older. This book is the perfect graduation gift or a special gift as your child becomes an adult.

The joy and laughter shared will be invaluable.

Melinda Pruitt,
Author

I Choose You...
From One Thousand Babies

Before you were born, I would close my eyes and
imagine your face.

I just couldn't wait to see you.

Parents, place your
pregnancy photo
here.

You finally arrived and I thanked God for such a beautiful baby.

I would look at you and my heart would melt.

Parents, place your
new born baby's
picture here.

At night I would whisper in your ear, "If God said pick any baby you want from a thousand babies, I would choose you."

Parents, place your
picture of mom or
dad holding baby
while sitting in a
rocking chair here.

Beautiful, sweet babies would surround me but you
would be the one I see.

Parents, place your
picture of baby and
parents together
here.

When I kissed your little face at night, I would say,

"I want no other baby but you," over and over again.

Parents, place your
picture of baby
sleeping in a crib
here.

You grew up much too fast; pulling yourself up, standing on your own, and like magic you were walking.

Parents, place your
picture of baby's first
steps here.

I love the pictures of you feeding yourself.

You would make such a mess.

Parents, place your
picture of baby
eating and making a
mess here.

You were smart, very smart. You would talk forever, and you knew so many different words.

Parents, place your
picture of your child
in pre-school here.

Your first day of kindergarten was scary for me, but you were brave. I was right there to pick you up after school. You ran into my arms, and we would say in unison...

I choose you.

Parents, place your
picture of your
child's first day of
kindergarten here.

Space for Additional
Special Photos

Space for Additional
Special Photos

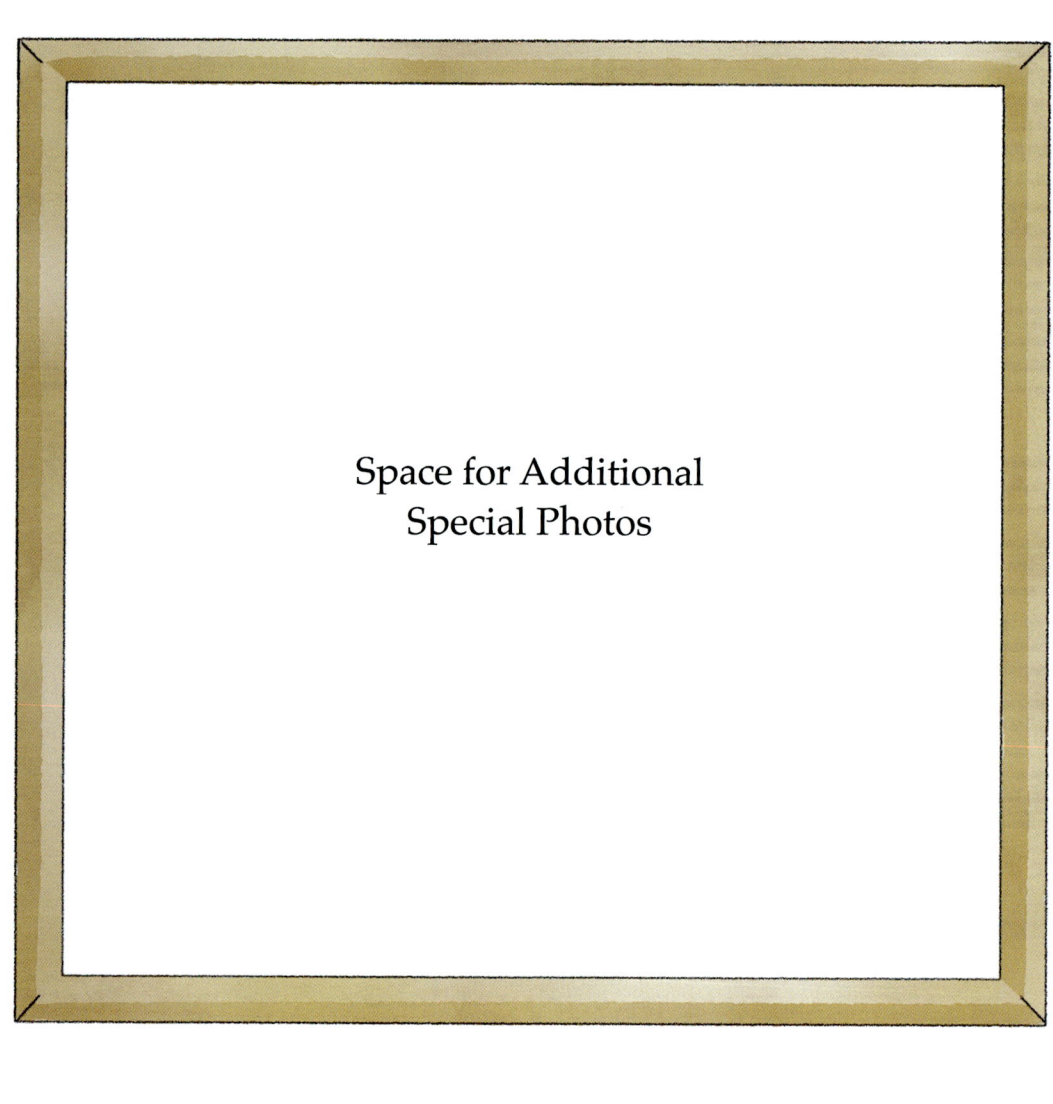

Space for Additional
Special Photos

Space for Additional
Special Photos

Space for Additional
Special Photos